The Sea Is Calling Me

Other poetry anthologies edited by
Lee Bennett Hopkins

The Sea Is Calling

Me

POEMS SELECTED BY **LEE BENNETT HOPKINS**

ILLUSTRATED BY **WALTER GAFFNEY-KESSELL**

HARCOURT BRACE JOVANOVICH, PUBLISHERS   San Diego New York London

Copyright © 1986 by Lee Bennett Hopkins

Illustrations copyright © 1986 by Walter Gaffney-Kessell

Printed in the United States of America

Designed by Barbara DuPree Knowles

LIBRARY OF CONGRESS CATALOGING IN PUBLICATION DATA
Main entry under title:
The Sea is calling me.
    Includes index.
    SUMMARY: A collection of poems by a variety of authors about the ocean, the seashore, lighthouses, seashells, sandcastles, and other objects associated with the sea.
    1. Sea poetry, American—Juvenile poetry. 2. Sea poetry, English—Juvenile poetry. 3. Children's poetry, American. 4. Children's poetry, English. [1. Sea poetry. 2. American poetry—Collections. 3. English poetry—Collections] I. Hopkins, Lee Bennett. II. Gaffney-Kessell, Walter, ill.
PS595.S39S4   1986   811'.008'036   85-16412
ISBN 0-15-271155-4

A B C D E
First Edition

Every effort has been made to trace the ownership of all copyrighted material and to secure the necessary permissions to reprint these selections. In the event of any question arising as to the use of any material, the editor and publisher, while expressing regret for any inadvertent error, will be happy to make the necessary correction in future printings.

    Thanks are due to the following for permission to reprint the copyrighted materials listed below:

ATHENEUM PUBLISHERS, INC., for "Until I Saw the Sea" from *I Feel the Same Way* by Lilian Moore. Copyright © 1967 by Lilian Moore. Reprinted with the permission of Atheneum Publishers.

CURTIS BROWN, LTD., for "On an August Day" by Lee Bennett Hopkins. Copyright © 1986 by Lee Bennett Hopkins; and for "Sunset Blues" from *No One Writes a Letter to the Snail* by Maxine Kumin. Text copyright © 1962 by Maxine Kumin. Both reprinted by permission of Curtis Brown, Ltd.

DOUBLEDAY & COMPANY, INC., for "I'd Like to Be a Lighthouse" from *Taxis and Toadstools* by Rachel Field. Copyright 1926 by Doubleday & Company, Inc. Reprinted by permission of the publisher.

HARCOURT BRACE JOVANOVICH, INC., for "maggie and molly and milly and may" from *Complete Poems 1913–1962* by E. E. Cummings. Copyright © 1956 by E. E. Cummings; and for three lines from "Sand Scribblings" in *Smoke and Steel* by Carl Sandburg, copyright 1920 by Harcourt Brace Jovanovich, Inc.; renewed 1948 by Carl Sandburg. Both reprinted by permission of Harcourt Brace Jovanovich, Inc.

HARPER & ROW, PUBLISHERS, INC., for "Waves of the Sea" from *Out in the Dark and Daylight: Poems* by Aileen Fisher. Text Copyright © 1980 by Aileen Fisher; for "Sitting in the Sand" from *Dogs & Dragons, Trees & Dreams: A Collection of Poems* by Karla Kuskin. Copyright © 1958 by Karla Kuskin; and for "The Sandpiper" from *River Winding: Poems* by Charlotte Zolotow (Thomas Y. Crowell Co.). Text Copyright © 1970 by Charlotte Zolotow. All reprinted by permission of Harper & Row, Publishers, Inc.

INSTRUCTOR for "Song for a Surf-Rider" by Sarah Van Alstyne Allen. Reprinted from *Instructor*, June 1966. Copyright © 1966 by The Instructor Publications, Inc. Used by permission.

BOBBI KATZ for "Sea Shore Shanty." Copyright © 1983 by Bobbi Katz. Used by permission of the author who controls all rights.

CONSTANCE ANDREA KEREMES for "Sand Castle" and "Ocean Treasures." Used by permission of the author who controls all rights.

SANDRA LIATSOS for "Seashell" and "At the Beach." Used by permission of the author who controls all rights.

MYRA COHN LIVINGSTON for "Wharf" from *A Crazy Flight and Other Poems* by Myra Cohn Livingston. Copyright © 1969 by Myra Cohn Livingston. Reprinted by permission of Marian Reiner for the author.

MODERN CURRICULUM PRESS, INC., for "Shell Castles" from *Songs From Around a Toadstool Table* by Rowena Bastin Bennett. Copyright © 1967 by Rowena Bastin Bennett. Used by permission of Modern Curriculum Press.

CHARLES SCRIBNER'S SONS for "Wild Day at the Shore" from *At the Top of My Voice and Other Poems* by Felice Holman. Copyright © 1970 by Felice Holman. Reprinted with the permission of Charles Scribner's Sons.

VIKING PENGUIN INC. for "Sea-Weed" by D. H. Lawrence from *Complete Poems*, collected and edited by Vivian de Sola Pinto and F. Warren Roberts. Copyright © 1964, 1971 by Angelo Ravagli and C. M. Weekley, Executors of the Estate of Frieda Lawrence Ravagli. Reprinted by permission of Viking Penguin Inc.

WALKER & COMPANY for "Tell Me, Tell Me, Sarah Jane" from *Figgie Hobbin* by Charles Causley. Copyright © 1973 by Charles Causley. Used by permission of the publisher, Walker & Company.

CHARLOTTE ZOLOTOW for "Summer Snow" from *All That Sunlight* by Charlotte Zolotow (Harper & Row). Copyright © 1967 by Charlotte Zolotow. Used by permission of the author who controls all rights.

FOR CHARLOTTE S. HUCK

who has sparked *so* many

to sail into poetry

Sea Shore Shanty BOBBI KATZ

Hermit crabs and cranberry plants,
Beach plum jelly to bring to your aunts,
Sand white—sea blue,
And nothing you really have to do.

Quahog pies that taste just right,
Bayberry candles to light at night,
Sand white—sea blue,
And nothing you really have to do.

Sandy castles with seaweed walls,
Pink pond lilies and wild duck calls,
Sand white—sea blue,
And nothing you really have to do.

Until I Saw the Sea LILIAN MOORE

Until I saw the sea
I did not know
that wind
could wrinkle water so.

I never knew
that sun
could splinter a whole sea of blue.

Nor
did I know before,
a sea breathes in and out
upon a shore.

8

Sitting in the Sand KARLA KUSKIN

Sitting in the sand and the sea comes up
So you put your hands together
And you use them like a cup
And you dip them in the water
With a scooping kind of motion
And before the sea goes out again
You have a sip of ocean.

9

On an August Day

LEE BENNETT HOPKINS

Ocean waves rush in
just in time
to give the shore-birds'
hot-burning legs
a cool, cool bath.

The Sandpiper

CHARLOTTE ZOLOTOW

Look at the little sandpiper
skittering along the sandy shore
such a little light thing
such a little bright thing
stenciling tiny clawprints
waves will wash away
                    once more.

maggie and milly and molly and may

E. E. CUMMINGS

maggie and milly and molly and may
went down to the beach(to play one day)

and maggie discovered a shell that sang
so sweetly she couldn't remember her troubles,and

milly befriended a stranded star
whose rays five languid fingers were;

and molly was chased by a horrible thing
which raced sideways while blowing bubbles:and

may came home with a smooth round stone
as small as a world and as large as alone.

For whatever we lose(like a you or a me)
it's always ourselves we find in the sea

Waves of the Sea AILEEN FISHER

Waves of the sea
make the sound of thunder
when they break against rocks
and somersault under.

Waves of the sea
make the sound of laughter
when they run down the beach
and birds run after.

Sea-Weed D. H. LAWRENCE

Sea-weed sways and sways and swirls
as if swaying were its form of stillness;
and if it flushes against fierce rock
it slips over it as shadows do, without hurting itself.

Song for a Surf-Rider

SARAH VAN ALSTYNE ALLEN

I ride the horse that is the sea.
His mane of foam flows wild and free.
His eyes flash with an emerald fire.
His mighty heart will never tire.
His hoofbeats echo on the sand.
He quivers as I raise my hand.
We race together, the sea and I,
Under the watching summer sky
To where the magic islands lie.

Wild Day at the Shore

FELICE HOLMAN

Upward a gull
Outward a tern
Upward and outward and seaward.
Inward the wind
Downward the waves
Inward and downward and leeward.
Wind, waves, and sky.
Gull, tern, and I.

Ocean Treasures

CONSTANCE ANDREA KEREMES

What treasures lie beneath
 the ocean waves?
Do magic creatures dwell
 in secret caves?
I'm sure that there's
 an octopus or two,
And one old whale who
 calls himself Big Blue.
Perhaps a fiddler crab
 plays his sweet tune,
While silv'ry fish blow bubbles
 as they croon.
And when the sea horse
 bows his noble head,
The baby mermaids
 all swim off to bed.

At the Beach

SANDRA LIATSOS

First I walked
the way
a sandpiper walks
quickly on my stick-legs.
Then I walked
a crab-walk
sideways across the sand.
Then I was a periwinkle
rolling in a wave
rolling onto land.
Then I was a sand-child
trailing home
through the trickly sand.

Sand Castle   CONSTANCE ANDREA KEREMES

Sandra built a castle out of sand.
Eddie, Juan, and Winnie lent a hand.
Winnie scooped out sand to make a moat.
In it Eddie placed a seashell boat.
Sandra built two turrets strong and tall,
Juan pressed pearl-white stones around each wall.
The children spoke of damsels and of knights,
And snow-white steeds and fiery dragon fights.
They sat and dreamed that sunny summer day
'Til high tide came and took their dreams away.

Shell Castles ROWENA BENNETT

A seashell is a castle
  Where a million echoes roam,
    A wee castle,
      Sea castle,
Tossed up by the foam;
  A wee creature's,
    Sea creature's
      Long deserted home.

Seashell SANDRA LIATSOS

This seashell is an ocean cove
That holds a liquid sound
Of waves that rush a hidden shore
Where stranger shells are found.
Shells that whisper secrets
Of how the ocean grew,
Shells that know which stories
Of the sea are really true.

Tell Me, Tell Me, Sarah Jane

CHARLES CAUSLEY

Tell me, tell me, Sarah Jane,
　　Tell me, dearest daughter,
Why are you holding in your hand
　　A thimbleful of water?
Why do you hold it to your eye
　　And gaze both late and soon
From early morning light until
　　The rising of the moon?

Mother, I hear the mermaids cry,
　　I hear the mermen sing,
And I can see the sailing ships
　　All made of sticks and string.
And I can see the jumping fish,
　　The whales that fall and rise
And swim about the waterspout
　　That swarms up to the skies.

Tell me, tell me, Sarah Jane,
  Tell your darling mother,
Why do you walk beside the tide
  As though you loved none other?
Why do you listen to a shell
  And watch the waters curl,
And throw away your diamond ring
  And wear instead a pearl?

Mother, I hear the water
  Beneath the headland pinned,
And I can see the sea gull
  Sliding down the wind.
I taste the salt upon my tongue
  As sweet as sweet can be.

Tell me, my dear, whose voice you hear?

  It is the sea, the sea.

Wharf MYRA COHN LIVINGSTON

There's that smell of the boats.
Sometimes you have to hold your nose
To keep it out, that smell;
But when it's keen, when it's stinking,
It gets you to thinking about the fishermen
Off the shore. The lobsters, snappers,
Baby pink shrimp, the albacore,
And how, with nets, the fishermen bob
  their boats
To sea. To sea. To catch the fish.

Summer Snow

CHARLOTTE ZOLOTOW

An evening by the sea
just before night
the fishing pier turned
a feathery white,
a lovely white, just as though
all those gulls
were summer snow.

from
Sand Scribblings

CARL SANDBURG

Boxes on the beach are empty.
Shake 'em and the nails loosen.
They have been somewhere.

I'd Like to Be
a Lighthouse

RACHEL FIELD

I'd like to be a lighthouse
    And scrubbed and painted white.
I'd like to be a lighthouse
    And stay awake all night
To keep my eye on everything
    That sails my patch of sea;
I'd like to be a lighthouse
    With the ships all watching me.

Sunset Blues

MAXINE W. KUMIN

Seagulls' crying
on the edge of town
over the harbor
when the sun goes down

makes the loneliest
kind of cry,
makes me ache
that the day's gone by,

stings my throat
and itches my nose.
Guess they think
when the old sun goes

that it falls in the sea
like a ripe beach plum,
that tomorrow is over
before it can come.

Guess they think
every sunset sky
is the world's last day
and it makes them cry.

Well, I know better.
The sun won't drown
But when seagulls rise
on the edge of town

and call through the harbor
Bad news! Bad news!
I always get
those sunset blues.

Index
OF AUTHORS,
TITLES, AND
FIRST LINES